You Are Gifted

Transformational Quotes That Bring Out the Gift and
Light from Within You Irrespective of Adversities

Nadia McInnis

authorHOUSE®

AuthorHouse™ UK
1663 Liberty Drive
Bloomington, IN 47403 USA
www.authorhouse.co.uk
Phone: 0800.197.4150

Published by AuthorHouse 07/19/2017

ISBN: 978-1-5246-8308-5 (sc)
ISBN: 978-1-5246-8307-8 (e)

Print information available on the last page.

Any people depicted in stock imagery provided by Thinkstock are models, and such images are being used for illustrative purposes only. Certain stock imagery © Thinkstock.

This book is printed on acid-free paper.

Because of the dynamic nature of the Internet, any web addresses or links contained in this book may have changed since publication and may no longer be valid. The views expressed in this work are solely those of the author and do not necessarily reflect the views of the publisher, and the publisher hereby disclaims any responsibility for them.

CONTENTS

INTRODUCTION

Throughout my life I have had many experiences, communicated with a lot of people, and observed many things that some will take a lifetime to discover. Others may have discovered them but could not put them into words or action; because of fear, uncertainties, low self esteem or a lack of self confidence. I will share my discoveries, observations, and most importantly, solutions, with you.

My aim is to help you discover your gift and shine your light for the world to see irrespective of adversities, situations, past experiences, present situations or people determined to see you fail.

I want to encourage every one of you reading this book to write your own personal quotes to live by and share with others. I am a firm believer in sharing the best I have with everyone who wants it. You never know what someone is going through, a word from you could prevent suicide or help a person who has failed choose not to accept this as a permanent situation. That is why I share everything I learn and know, nothing is too good for me to share with anyone. The more I share my knowledge, the more knowledge I receive from God.

As you read and meditate on these quotes, you will discover the light inside you, you will become illuminated, your eyes and understanding will be opened to your true potential, and if you take action, then one day I will be reading your story of prosperity.

Quotes became very important to me after falling asleep one night whilst listening to a message from Dr Myles Munroe. I woke up the next day with a quote on my mind. I felt like it was just for me, it was so perfect for how I was feeling and it helped get me out of bondage and enter into my true destination - using my gift and shining my light for the world to see. I know the quote was given to me personally by God Himself, and it is the first quote I am going to share with you. I got up and wrote it down because it was so personal to me, and then I started to write several motivational quotes to help people who were going through the same or similar situations. Quotes also became important to me when I was going through a challenging time in my life and all I could do was talk to God and write done my observations and solutions.

I wrote many quotes to encourage others to shine and I will leave them with you. I am sure that you will find one or many that will help you at each point of your life as you embark on your mission to discover your gift and shine your light for the world to see.

NEVER FORGET THAT YOUR PAST DOES NOT DECREASE YOUR VALUE.

Nadia McInnis

London

"BE THE CATERPILLAR THAT
DEVELOPS INTO A BUTTERFLY,
NO LONGER TRAMPLED ON BUT
CHERISHED AND WATCHED."

~Nadia McInnis~

I found out the hard way - or should I say the perfect way - that wisdom was better than acting foolishly. A good man without wisdom and boldness is fully exposed, but a good man with wisdom and boldness who can stop him? A good man must also be a very wise man, lest his goodness be trampled upon - it will be like that man did nothing well.

The Bible says, "...Cast not your pearls before swines, lest they trample them under their feet and turn around and rend you." ~Matthew 7:6~

"DO NOT EXPECT THOSE AROUND YOU TO HOST A PARTY FOR YOU AS YOU AIM FOR THE SKY. YOU MUST ENCOURAGE YOURSELF."

~Nadia McInnis~

You will discover, or have already discovered, that as you make the transition from the person you are to the person you know you were born to become, that many people who are close to you, that you expect would be willing to support you, will not - and some will also tell others not to. This will not be easy for you to handle when you first discover it, and many give up at this stage because it becomes a lonely, frustrating journey.

A great way to encourage yourself is to know and understand that it is a part of the process and it was made to be that way so that no man can take credit for your success. Also, remember that at this stage, God is closer to you than ever before, because all you have is Him.

*"GREAT IDEAS ROAM AROUND
WAITING TO BE CAUGHT BY
RUNNERS. YOUR IDEAS ARE
NOT PRIVATE - RUN NOW."*

~Nadia McInnis~

How many times have you been in a room and an idea comes to mind? Maybe you were too afraid to speak it out or pursue it. You sit in silence as someone gets up and voices the same idea while everyone commends them. You are left feeling frustrated because you had the same idea but did nothing.

When an idea comes to you, ensure that you act IMMEDIATELY and see it through to completion because it is not just for you but is to help people – even some not yet born. When you get an idea that you feel really passionate about act immediately because that idea has its season and time. Also, whoever pursues the idea and completes it gets the reward.

"BRING OUT YOUR GIFT, THE WORLD IS WAITING FOR IT."

~Nadia McInnis~

Each of us has something special that was given to us by God. For some it is speaking, some singing, some planning, some dancing, some acting, some teaching, some writing, some running, some creating and the list goes on.

What do you do with that gift?

What you should not do is keep it inside of you hidden, for no one to see. Always remember that even though it is your GIFT from God it is also your GIFT to the world. God does nothing without a reason, he gave you a gift for you to be a blessing. It is while being a blessing you are blessed even more.

There are songs I listen to from time to time that bring me so much joy and peace, the writers seem to know exactly how I was feeling without ever meeting me. This is because that gift of writing or singing was not just for them but for the entire world. If it was just for them, then only they would have been blessed by their gift. We all have gifts to help. So, bring out your gift - the world is waiting for it.

"YOU CAN STOP A MAN FROM SHARING HIS DREAMS WITH YOU, BUT YOU CANNOT STOP HIM FROM BUILDING IT WITHOUT YOU."

~Nadia McInnis~

Resilience is a vital part of bringing out your gift and shining your light for the world to see.

You may try to share your dreams with others, in the beginning, thinking that they may be interested in helping you, but only to find out that their only interest is in you doing what is best for them. What do you do? This is when you start to build your dreams by yourself because you are not by yourself, God is with you every step of the way. Ensure that you do not stop building.

*"YOU WILL NEVER KNOW
WHAT YOU CAN DO UNTIL YOU
TRY, AND YOU WILL NEVER
KNOW HOW MUCH YOU CAN
ACHIEVE UNTIL YOU START."*

~Nadia McInnis~

Have you ever been a part of a group that you know you should not be a part of, but because of the length of time you have been with them, and the connections you share, you find it difficult to leave? You refuse to leave the group even when it is clear to you, and all around you, that the group is hurting you more than helping you. This is because change is hard but inevitable for success.

Change is hard because it is unfamiliar and we love the familiar. This is why companies employ change managers when they want to introduce something new. Employers believe the change managers can help the employees to respond better. However irrespective of how hard change is, it is necessary for growth.

"UNTIL YOU START YOU WILL NEVER KNOW HOW YOU WILL FINISH."

~Nadia McInnis~

Never assume that because others you know have failed doing what you are attempting to do, you will fail as well. This is completely and utterly false. There was a time that I used to look at committed church-going people and tell myself that if that man or woman is not prosperous, but instead experiencing a very unattractive life, then how can I be prosperous?

I used this to judge my progress until the Holy Spirit revealed to me that I should never compare myself with anyone based on what I see and hear. I can only see those things which they choose to show me. Since that day I have never compared or judged my progress with anyone irrespective of who they claim to be. I decided to act when God tells me to act, irrespective of if others doing similar things are succeeding and failing. I am confident that my own story will be better.

"IF YOU KNOW YOU HAVE SOMETHING GREAT TO OFFER, THEN BE BOLD AND CONFIDENT ABOUT IT. BEING BOLD AND CONFIDENT PAYS."

~Nadia McInnis~

Many people who have little, or nothing to offer, are bold and confident; so why are you afraid when you have something great to offer? I have met many business men and women who continue to surprise me with their lack of knowledge and poor services - yet some are making huge profits. This to me is a tragedy for the man who has excellent products and services, yet still, no one knows about him.

I discovered that one of the reasons for this is that some people are very bold and confident about the rubbish they are offering. They are so bold and confident that people believe in what they say they have. Your confidence will come with practice, look people in the eyes and speak confidently about your great product or services and never give up.

"PAY ATTENTION TO KNOWLEDGE OR PAY FOR YOUR IGNORANCE."

~Nadia McInnis~

As you embark on your journey to success, you will find all sorts of people charging huge sums of money for simple information you can get for free. Spend time reading and listening to real experts in your area and do some study for yourself.

Ignorance is very expensive but the application of the right knowledge is power. Some of the best knowledge that I have received for my business to move it to a higher level I was given for free. However, I have also paid for information that produced nothing.

"THE ROAD TO VICTORY REQUIRES CONSTANT FOCUS, CONCENTRATE ON YOUR DESTINATION."

~Nadia McInnis~

One day, as I was driving on a street and rushing to my destination, a car from a side road was trying to push in front my car. I was rushing so I did not want to let the driver in. I did not even realise when I stopped looking in front of me and was completely focused on the driver. I was so busy trying to stop him that my car started to go in his direction. I suddenly noticed that my car was turning towards the driver instead of continuing where I had intended to go. I had to quickly adjust it to my destination and continue my journey without looking at the driver anymore.

It was in that moment I discovered that so many people have derailed because they got distracted by obstacles they should have ignored. Just continue your journey and leave the obstacles alone, they will sort themselves out.

"BE UNSTOPPABLE AND IMMOVABLE, YOUR SUCCESS IS WORTH IT."

~Nadia McInnis~

Let nothing stop you from moving forward - no situation, family, friends, or adversities stop you from achieving your goals. There is so much joy in success and perseverance after you have achieved something you have always wanted. Once you persevere and achieve a goal you will want to do so much more. It is very important to remember that the lessons you learn in the process are priceless, they can only be fully understood by experience.

"BE CONFIDENT IN YOUR ABILITIES, THERE IS NO ONE LIKE YOU."

~Nadia McInnis~

We are all gifted in our own ways and with our own unique talents. It does not matter how insignificant it appears to you or to some around you. Do not worry about that - it is your gift, not theirs. You need to know that you bring something unique and special to this world, and you must be confident about it. Become confident in it, use it, develop it and let it shine all over the world. No gift or ability you have is useless, but you need to believe in it and the one who gave it to you. It was given to you for a reason, which is to give to others, to help them recognize theirs also and be blessed.

"IT DOES NOT MATTER HOW MANY PEOPLE HAVE TRIED AND FAILED, YOU ARE UNIQUE: TRY IT YOURSELF."

~Nadia McInnis~

See with the eyes of God by believing what He tells you about what you can do. It does not matter about your educational level, or the example of others who have failed despite their qualifications, if you know you were created to do something then keep doing it until you succeed. Only use the word of God as a guide and not another man's failure or life to judge your gift.

*"YOU SHOULD CONFUSE
DREAM KILLERS WITH YOUR
RESILIENCE, THEY HAVE NOT
SEEN A FRACTION OF YOU YET."*

~Nadia McInnis~

I am convinced that some people spend most of their time planning for others to fail. They will try everything they can do to make you fail and not accomplish your dreams. Each time you pause to reassess they think you have given up. Never give up. If you fall, then rise again and go further next time. With each effort push a little further, become better than before until you become the best. Learn from your past mistakes and get better. This will confuse and frustrate the dream killers because they will never know where you are coming from and what you are coming with.

*"FORGET ABOUT WHAT PEOPLE
SAID ABOUT YOU, TODAY IS
A NEW DAY: WHAT ARE YOU
DOING ABOUT YOU?"*

~Nadia McInnis~

Too often, we waste our precious thoughts and voices talking about what people have done to us and said about us. Let me assure you that the talking and lies against you will not stop. In fact, the more you achieve and the more popular you become, the more they will talk and lie about you.

Every day make up your mind to do what you were born to do, give it your best and give no attention to negativity. Let them do what they think they were born to do while you excel doing what you were born to do, and let us see who will leave a legacy.

*"SHOW LOVE AT ALL TIMES,
IT WILL MAKE YOU FEEL
BETTER AT ALL TIMES."*

~Nadia McInnis~

It can be difficult to show love at all times when the people who are demanding it are the most manipulative and selfish people you know. Remember that our command was not to love those who are good to us, but everyone. When you show love in the midst of hatred towards you, you have peace and joy that no billionaire can buy. Your eyes will be opened to so many great opportunities that hate and revenge block.

*"JUST WHEN YOU THOUGHT
THAT YOU GOT IT RIGHT,
YOU FOUND OUT THAT YOU
ARE STILL LEARNING AND
IMPROVING. LEARNING AND
IMPROVING NEVER STOP."*

~Nadia McInnis~

Sometimes on your journey to fulfil your purpose you will learn so much, maybe to the point where you feel like you have seen or heard it all. But something will happen to make you realise that you are still at the beginning. When this happens, it is not time to get discouraged and give up. Just make the necessary adjustments; keep learning, keep adjusting and keep growing. Learning truly never stops.

*"WHEN BUILDING YOUR DREAMS,
DO NOT WAIT FOR PEOPLE
TO BRING THE BRICKS,
GET UP, GET BUSY AND TAKE
CONTROL OF YOUR LIFE."*

~Nadia McInnis~

Sometimes, in the beginning of a mission, you will assume that close relatives and friends will help you out along the way because it seems natural to you. You would and have helped them.

Very soon you will find out that many will not help - even when it costs them nothing to do so. The thing to do is to start doing ALL that you can do and keep moving. Stop assuming and waiting. If you are unsure about their position then ask them and watch to see if you get the support you crave, and if you don't, move along swiftly - help is literally on the way!

"WHAT DO YOU NEED TO CHANGE TO CHANGE YOUR LIFE? CHANGE IT."

~Nadia McInnis~

There are many habits that are natural to us but are also very detrimental to our success. You need to find out what these bad habits are and change them if you want to see real progress. Don't just accept them and say this is how I am, I have been like this since I was born. Are you selfish, or are you unfriendly or a perpetual liar? You may have been doing these things for years but it is important to change them for proper growth to take place. They will not all be easy to change but if you want to see great results then change is inevitable.

No one said it was easy but it is compulsory to change to elevate your position.

"YOU WILL MAKE IT, JUST KEEP MOVING."

~Nadia McInnis~

At times you will want to give up for so many reasons. Things just aren't working out how you planned them. There seems to be no money, no assistance and no director or direction. The only thing to do in this situation are the things which you can do, costing you nothing but your time. You may be surprised with how these things pay off in your journey.

But do not stop or neglect to do the things that you are able to do yourself. Yes, you will need help but there are many things you can do on your own as you get started.

"DO NOT KEEP QUIET REGARDING YOUR FUTURE, MAKE SURE YOU TELL YOUR OWN STORY."

~Nadia McInnis~

I have seen gifted and talented people with so much to offer to the world, but no one knows about them. They dedicate their lives to only working on other people's dreams and hide all their gifts and talents hoping that one day that person will open a million-dollar door for them - while that person is also looking for someone to open that door for them.

There is nothing wrong with dedicating some time to helping another man fulfil his dreams, I have done so for several years and I am still doing so. In fact, my entire life is to help people discover and use their gifts. But if that is not your calling then you should have a time to serve and a time to lead in your area of gifting. **Set a date when you will start working on your dreams completely with no distraction.**

"FORGET PAST MISTAKES, LOOK TO THE FUTURE - IT IS IN YOUR HANDS."

~Nadia McInnis~

Too many people keep thinking about their past mistakes and what they should have changed and all the people who hindered them several years ago. You can never undo the past but you can CERTAINLY make the future the way you want it to be. In order to do this, you cannot keep blaming your past.

Only refer to the past when you are using it as a testimony to help others see the progress you have made so that they too will be inspired by your progress and transformation. Your past is to help others to overcome what you have already overcome; it is not for you to keep thinking and complaining about. THE FUTURE IS BRIGHT AND NEW, IT IS YOURS TO TAKE.

"WHEN YOU FIND YOUR GIFT,
YOU WILL FIND YOUR PURPOSE.
WHEN YOU FULFIL YOUR PURPOSE,
YOU WILL BE SATISFIED."

~Nadia McInnis~

When I discovered that my gift was speaking, I immediately knew that my purpose was to transform millions through my voice. As soon as I started to help others through my voice I found out what real joy and fulfilment felt like. Not just because I am helping people, but know that I am also helping myself. This is because I am walking in purpose and it brings me happiness and blessings.

Endeavour to discover and maximize your gift because that is where true everlasting satisfaction lies.

*"YOU MIGHT FEEL LIKE GIVING UP
ON YOUR DREAMS. DO NOT GIVE
UP, THERE IS AN UNEXPLAINABLE
JOY WAITING FOR YOU."*

~Nadia McInnis~

As you go towards your dreams, there will be many times that you feel like giving up. Sometimes because of no progress, no help, family pressure, no seen results, no guidance, you name it. These things will happen. Let me assure you that when you keep moving forward and you GO GET your first reward you will be so pleased and motivated that it brings an abundance of joy and confidence to keep going.

You need to understand that tough times may still come but it will make you tougher. Just keep taking one step at a time. Keep on and experience that joy of accomplishment.

"THE WORLD WILL NOT PUSH YOU TO MOVE. WHEN YOU PUSH YOURSELF THE WORLD WILL FOLLOW."

~Nadia McInnis~

This is one of my personal favourites because I have seen it so many times. When you begin to shine your light and use your gift, many will not cheer you, encourage you or even tell you to keep going. You will get absolutely no support or word of encouragement from many people around you. If you are experiencing a lack of support you may feel like you are wasting your time but when those same people see you prospering they are the first to copy you, ask for your help and demand you share what you have earned.

Do help them all if you can but remember where you got your strength from in those times and draw closer to that source because that source will never leave, but instead, keep pouring into you.

"YOUR DREAMS ARE YOUR REALITY. YOU MUST WIN - JUST DO IT."

~Nadia McInnis~

Never believe your dreams are just wishful thinking and will not become a reality. Every invention and creation was once someone's dream. You can make them a reality if you pray, plan, take bold ACTION and let God use you.

"IF YOU SHOUT LOUD ENOUGH
THEY WILL HEAR YOU, BUT
IF YOU KEEP QUIET, NO
ONE WILL HEAR YOU."

~Nadia McInnis~

Stop hiding your abilities in your house or under another man's vision. Help can be so very close to you, but because you are so quiet and conscious of your flaws, help cannot find you. Become brave and loud with your gift and let the world see and hear it. You will eventually reap the reward if you stick with it long enough. I heard someone say that your 10% is someone's 100% so give what you've got.

"GO AFTER YOUR DREAMS WITH EVERYTHING YOU'VE GOT AND HAVEN'T GOT."

~Nadia McInnis~

As you set out on your mission to achieve your goals, there are many things you will discover about yourself. You will discover things you never knew you had in you and things you never knew you could do.

Sometimes, you will also believe that you just do not have what it takes to become successful. However, you must remember that the God who gave it to you is also able to provide help with the things you do not have. The important thing is to never stop, just keep focused and keep moving.

"CHALLENGES COME NOT TO STEP ON YOU BUT FOR YOU TO STEP ON AND REACH HIGHER."

~Nadia McInnis~

I am so sure about this. Can you believe that I achieve more, do more and focus more in challenging times? Somehow, the challenges get me going. When others are crying and complaining about challenges I am propelled to work harder, do more and achieve greater things. There is so much pleasure in success in the midst of challenges. Let me say that again - there is so much pleasure in success in the midst of challenges!

Of course, you might cry sometimes, of course you might complain sometimes, but quickly dust yourself off and start working harder than before. Challenges should be used as motivation, not a hindrance.

"DO NOT GET WEARY, THE JOURNEY CANNOT BE COMPARED TO THE JOY AHEAD - KEEP GOING."

~Nadia McInnis~

Yes, there are lonely times. The path of a leader and a great man can be very lonely. Of course you will feel weary and tired, but if you need to take a few minutes break then take some time out to think and relax.

When I gave birth to my first child, I was in labour for twenty hours and I believed that it was the most severe pain I would ever feel. I kept telling my husband that I was going to die and that I could not take the pain anymore. It was far greater than I had ever imagined. After twenty hours of constant pain, I had my son and all the pain disappeared as my joy replaced the pain. I would go through that pain again and again for the joy I received. Your success is worth so much more than your current struggles. You are just in labour preparing for the greatness that you are about to give birth to.

"HAVE CONFIDENCE IN WHAT YOU ARE MADE OF - YOU ARE GIFTED."

~Nadia McInnis~

Too often we feel like we are not good enough. We feel too fat, too ugly, too uneducated, our accent is not acceptable or we do not look or sound like others who have made it in the area we are trying to pursue. All these excuses are lies. Great people went forward when they could have used one or more of these excuses to stay in mediocrity. They never regretted overcoming their shortcomings. Have confidence in ALL that you are because God knew you before you were born, He gave you your gift. Fix what you can fix while you are working on your dreams, but don't wait another moment.

"DON'T JUST GROW OLDER GROW SMARTER. DON'T MAKE THE SAME OLD MISTAKES EVERY YEAR."

~Nadia McInnis~

I see this so often - people get older but not wiser. They keep falling into the same traps over and over again.

When I was a young girl adults would tell me that the older I got the wiser I would become. When I got older, I found out that belief was completely and totally false. To increase in age has nothing to do with an increase in wisdom. Age gives you experience but not wisdom, what do you do with the experiences you have had? How have you used them to improve your life and not make the same mistakes again?

"YOU SHOULD NOT FAIL, IT IS UP TO YOU."

~Nadia McInnis~

You will encounter many disappointments from people who promised to do things for you, businesses who promised to work with you and then decided to back out after you had made plans. Those disappointments are not enough to make you give up, learn from them and do it better next time. Your success or failure is completely up to your perseverance and not accepting no for an answer when you know that there is a yes in store.

"IF YOU ONLY KNEW WHAT YOU'VE GOT YOU WOULD HAVE LAUGHED AT THE ENEMY."

~Nadia McInnis~

Sometimes I see people quit because of temporary hindrances. They gave up because no one believed in them, supported them or they asked for a loan to grow their business and did not get it. You must remember that you have a God that is the biggest and the greatest. This is no reason to give up, become aware of the fact that God who gave you your gift is with you and no one has the power to destroy what he has deposited in you. Look adversities in the face and say, "I am bigger than you, you are too small."

"THEY THOUGHT THE CUT WOULD HAVE KILLED YOU, BUT INSTEAD, IT BROUGHT OUT YOUR GIFT."

~Nadia McInnis~

I was once part of an organisation where one of the leaders, who made most of the decisions, would do everything in her power to make me look incompetent and feel insignificant. This was very painful because I endured it for several years until I could not endure it anymore. The constant belittling and manipulation of myself and others drove me to create a great enterprise which put me in charge.

Sometimes we need to be cut where it really hurts so that we can go and create what we are supposed to create.

"IF YOU DON'T KNOW WHERE YOU ARE GOING THEY WILL SEND YOU EVERYWHERE. KNOW YOUR PURPOSE."

~Nadia McInnis~

A man who does not have a plan and a destination will be sent everywhere by those who have their own plans and destinations. He will constantly be used by others to do their errands and jobs while these people do the things that are important to them.

Most of the people giving you errands do not care about your future or if you have any plans to get there. How do you know? Ask them for help to fulfil your dreams; they will tell you to serve them because you aren't ready to go out on your own. Some die never ready - you will never be ready until you start.

"GREAT PEOPLE FULFIL THEIR MISSIONS REGARDLESS OF THE CHALLENGES THEY ENCOUNTER ALONG THE WAY."

~Nadia McInnis~

One day I was watching football and there was something I noticed that happened to some of the players as they were about to score. In one case, an opponent would come behind and try to grab the players foot, another opponent pulled down a player's shorts. One would jump on the back of the player and even fake being injured just to distract him. I also observed that the opponents did not even care if they got sent out of the match once they had succeeded in stopping the player from scoring the goal.

For me, what was most important was not the distraction of the opponents but the determination and focus of the man with the ball. Nothing and no one were strong enough to take his eyes off the goal. Remember the clock is ticking, and if you allow the distraction to waste your time the referee will blow the whistle ending the match before you score your goal. So run to your goal and do not look to the left or right. Keep running, keep moving and I will see you at the top.

"USE THE EXPERIENCES OF YOUR PAST TO MAKE BETTER DECISIONS BUT DO NOT LIVE IN YOUR PAST IF YOU WANT TO MOVE FORWARD."

~Nadia McInnis~

It may seem comforting to think about the past hurts, mistakes, betrayals, could have or if not's but the truth about dwelling on the past is that it will only make you bitter not better. Take a lesson or more from past mistakes and misfortunes and move on with more wisdom and determination.

"WHAT IF YOU FOUND OUT THAT IT WAS IMPOSSIBLE FOR YOU TO FAIL: WOULD YOU GO AFTER YOUR DREAMS WITH EVERYTHING YOU'VE GOT?"

~Nadia McInnis~

So many times, people give up too early because they thought they were about to fail and they tried to avoid disappointment. Some people feel better if they do not try as they may avoid failure. They have convinced themselves that not experiencing failure is better than experiencing it. The truth however is if you truly want to be successful then you have to be willing to fail, learn from it and do better next time. Every successful person has failed at some point and had to learn from it and move on.

*"YOU WILL MAKE SOME PAINFUL
DECISIONS ON YOUR WAY TO
SUCCESS. REMEMBER, IT'S
MORE PAINFUL IF YOU DON'T
MAKE THOSE DECISIONS."*

~Nadia McInnis~

Do not get too comfortable with people and behaviours that will not make your life better. You will have to get rid of some close friends and bad habits to get to a higher level. You have to get rid of people that do not encourage you but distract you; you have to get rid of oversleeping and spending many hours watching movies and having idle conversations with friends. It can be painful and lonely to drop them but the pain of permanent failure is worse. The pain of what you could have achieved, but were too distracted or too weak to achieve, is far worst, and most importantly, remember that your gift is not yours, people are waiting for it to release their gifts.

"DO NOT DIM YOUR LIGHTS TO PLEASE ANYONE - STARS SHINE."

~Nadia McInnis~

Some people will try to make you feel bad for standing out from the crowd or for trying too hard, but that's ok. They will say words to discourage you or make you feel like you are too passionate and you need to cool down. Do not turn down for anyone. That is not your business, your business is to shine your light for the world to see and GLORIFY your Father who is in heaven. THAT IS THE COMMAND FROM GOD.

"IF YOU BELIEVE AND TAKE BOLD STEPS, YOUR LIFE WILL CHANGE AND SURPRISE YOU."

~Nadia McInnis~

I cannot over emphasise the importance of confidence in pursuing your goals. Always have an, "I am great" attitude doing the things that great people do and watch your life change and surprise you as you think and act.

> *"DO NOT BE AFRAID TO PURSUE YOUR DREAMS BECAUSE OF WHAT OTHERS MAY SAY ABOUT YOU. BE AFRAID OF WHAT MIGHT HAPPEN TO OTHERS IF YOU DON'T PURSUE YOUR DREAMS."*

~Nadia McInnis~

Think about all the products you are using today. Think about all the services you are enjoying too because someone was not afraid to pursue their dreams, someone was not afraid to answer their calling. You have a product that someone is waiting for, you have a service that someone is waiting for, and even you, you are waiting to be fulfilled. Don't be afraid to pursue your dreams because of what others may say about you, be afraid of what may happen to others if you do not pursue your dreams.

*"THE PEOPLE YOU NEED TO HELP
YOU REACH YOUR DESTINATION
ARE AVAILABLE. SEEK THEM."*

~Nadia McInnis~

Many times when you start out on your mission to fulfil your purpose you will feel like there is no one who gets your vision or has your passion and no one is willing to walk with you to help you get there faster and easier. It will appear that way because that is how it is sometimes. However, as you continue to move forward you will find people who share your passion and your dreams, people who are willing to support you - so do not stop. Do all that you can do and leave no stone unturned.

"WHERE YOU ARE COMING FROM DOESN'T MATTER, TELL ME WHERE YOU ARE GOING."

~Nadia McInnis~

Never ever think that your past experiences are enough to destroy the future you are dreaming of. I was the happiest woman on earth when I found out that bad experiences or a bad past do not decrease my value or have any negative effect on my future; except the fact that it makes you stronger. Talk about where you are going and make plans to get there. Your future is new, bright and waiting for you to shine in it.

*"PEOPLE WILL TREAT YOU
HOW YOU ALLOW THEM TO,
TAKE CONTROL OF YOUR
LIFE OR THE WORLD WILL
TAKE CONTROL FOR YOU."*

~Nadia McInnis~

When you discover your value it becomes extremely difficult to stay around those people who do not value you.

You do not have to be rude or get angry when someone constantly disrespects you. You can confront them in a meek manner and voice your observation but ensure that you do not allow them to mistreat you. Do not sit back and say nothing. Do not keep quiet, because if you do, it will get worst and lead to frustration. Let them know your observations and try to find a solution if there is a solution. if not, leave them alone. Do not let them make you frustrated and bitter. Frustration leads to bitterness.

*"LIVE YOUR DREAMS AND
NOT SOMEONE ELSE DREAMS,
LEARN FROM OTHERS BUT
DO NOT BECOME THEM."*

~Nadia McInnis~

Good mentors are great, and you should copy them and learn what is necessary to become the success you are. But do not abandon your goals and take on their responsibility because you admire them. It is OK to serve and help them but there comes a time that you need to go and DO what you were born to do and leave your own legacy. If they object then you need to leave them behind. This only reveals their selfishness.

"NO ONE CAN DESTROY YOUR GIFT WITHOUT YOUR PERMISSION. MAKE WISE DECISIONS."

~Nadia McInnis~

Do not get to the point where, because you did what you were asked to, or went where you were asked to go, you failed to fulfil your own dreams and ambitions. This is why it is important to find out what your purpose is so that you can boldly say yes to things that benefit you and no to things that divert from your path. It is up to you, so be bold and confident about what you are about and tell those around you your aim. Dr Myles Munroe said that anyone who tries to distract you from your purpose is not a friend but an enemy.

"LIFE IS GOOD WHEN YOU ARE IN CONTROL: TAKE CONTROL OF YOUR LIFE."

~Nadia McInnis~

When you take control of your life by doing what you know is right and rejecting what you know is not right for you, your feelings of importance increases. You become more confident in yourself and what you are about. So take control back from the manipulators and lead your life to victory.

"CONFIDENCE IS AN IMPORTANT TRAIT TO HAVE TO EXCEL, BE CONFIDENT IN YOU SO YOU CAN BOLDLY TELL THE WORLD WHO YOU ARE."

-Nadia McInnis-

If you are struggling to believe in yourself no one will believe in you. Confidence also comes from experience and knowledge that there is something unique and special about what you have. Spend quality time practicing in front of people and gaining as much experience as you can in your area of gifting. It will make you bold and confident when displaying your talents.

"WHEN YOU BEGIN TO FULFIL YOUR PURPOSE, YOU BEGIN TO LIVE."

~Nadia McInnis~

There is no greater joy to me than the joy of doing what you were born to do and seeing the great results that it brings in people's lives and in your own life. There is an unexplainable joy from way down in your belly that makes everything beautiful and gives you complete satisfaction and fulfilment.

"DO NOT APOLOGIZE FOR YOUR GREATNESS. GREAT PEOPLE STAND OUT - BE UNSTOPPABLE."

~Nadia McInnis~

Be unstoppable; let nothing cause you to hide. Every great person had to step out of the pack. Some people may not like it but that is not your business.

"YOU DO NOT NEED PERMISSION FROM ANYONE TO BE GREAT. ONLY YOUR PERMISSION IS REQUIRED."

~Nadia McInnis~

Do not wait for anyone to validate your calling or your purpose. If God has said that is who you are, then that is who you are. They do not have to see it or accept it, it is your assignment - not theirs. Just walk in that direction. It does not matter if your pastor or mentor does not see that greatness in you. You are who God says you are. As you move in that direction and succeed they will eventually congratulate you.

*"THE EXCITEMENT OF
ACHIEVING YOUR PERSONAL
GOALS FAR EXCEEDS THE
WORK YOU PUT INTO IT."*

~Nadia McInnis~

That joy, that peace, that sense of satisfaction and achievement when you get the results you wanted is a fantastic feeling.

I know the work can feel hard, I know the push can be painful, but as soon as you get there all that pain and hard work will seem like nothing. You will be so glad you continued.

*"DOING THE RIGHT THING
IS ALWAYS THE BEST OPTION,
DO NOT LET ANYONE FORCE
YOU TO BECOME THE
PERSON YOU AREN'T."*

~Nadia McInnis~

Many times you will feel like you want to retaliate to negative people just to prove to them and others that they are wrong and you are right. It is tempting to retaliate but it is not necessary. To answer back exposes pride. There is something that can speak louder and that is your success. Some people want you to retaliate to try and disgrace you. Do not give them that pleasure; let God do the talking for you. No one can talk after God speaks.

"OFFENCE IS AN ENDLESS DETOUR, DO NOT LET IT TAKE YOU OFF YOUR PATH TO SUCCESS. THE MOST SUCCESSFUL PEOPLE DO NOT GIVE ANY ATTENTION TO NEGATIVITY."

-Nadia McInnis-

No matter what people say or what they try to do, do not give them any of your attention because you need all of it to get to your destination. Every offence is a plan by the enemy to lead you to destruction. Do not even think about it for a second. Remember, the Bible says that offence must surely come, but you have already won.

"I AM ON MY WAY TO VICTORY, DO NOT DISTRACT ME."

~Nadia McInnis~

Keep your objective always in sight and let nothing and no one distract you.

"WHATEVER YOU FOCUS ON PULLS YOU TOWARDS IT. WHERE WILL YOU END THE DAY?"

~Nadia McInnis~

Your mind is a powerful thing and what you think about will affect your actions. It has a subtle and unnoticeable way of moving your thoughts away from what you set out to do. You must consciously know what you are thinking about at all times. Make it a deliberate practice to keep your mind on the right thing. Always know why you are thinking about what you are thinking about. Because soon you will get to what you have been thinking about. It will not be long before your thoughts influence your actions. Whatever you think about you end up doing.

"CONCERNING YOUR GIFTS: DO NOT HESITATE, THE GIFT GIVER HAS PLANNED THE JOURNEY."

~Nadia McInnis~

There can be so many questions about how you will accomplish your purpose. But let me assure you that God Almighty has already prepared the way for you, so do not worry. Just ensure that you do ALL you are meant to do and never stop.

"KEEP IMPROVING YOUR GIFT. THE MORE YOU IMPROVE IT, THE MORE SUCCESS YOU WILL HAVE."

~Nadia McInnis~

Do not get to the point where you become complacent with your achievements or with what you think you have achieved. Do not think you know all that you need to know. God is full of ideas and inventions, and He is capable of teaching you new things every day; to make you someone the world has never seen before or will ever see again. Master everything He teaches you and he will continue to show you greater and mightier things.

"I AM JUST A HAPPY PERSON APPRECIATING MYSELF, NOTHING CAN CHANGE THAT."

~Nadia McInnis~

Some people may ask you, why are you so happy? Why are you always smiling as if you don't have problems? Well, they are right, your confidence in God makes you problem and worry free. Keep shouting joy, keep smiling because you know what God has done and is doing for you.

"WHETHER YOU BELIEVE IN ME OR NOT, I AM STILL HAPPY AND I AM STILL A SUCCESS."

~Nadia McInnis~

Some people will not believe in who you say you are. But the good news is, whether they believe in you or not, you are still a success and you are still blessed. Nothing can change that but you. Never decide to quit because someone does not believe in your gift, eventually, they will not need to believe, they will KNOW THAT YOU ARE WHO YOU SAY YOU ARE.

"DISAPPOINTMENTS CAN EITHER DESTROY YOUR DREAMS OR DEVELOP YOUR DREAMS - THE CHOICE IS YOURS."

~Nadia McInnis~

Some people experience disappointment when they had high expectations and gave up, never to recover. It could be a death in the family, physical and mental abuse, misfortunes, accidents, failures, you name it, some never recover from many of these things. While some, despite all the above and more, continue to push past the pain and are determined to win. Which way will you choose? I choose to win and win BIG. I will never give up until I am dead, and I will only die after I have emptied myself to everyone I am sent to.

"LOVE IS A MUST, RESPECT IS NECESSARY, BUT GIVE NO ONE CONTROL OF YOUR DESTINY."

~Nadia McInnis~

Let no man or leader deceive you that loving and respecting them is to always do what they want you to. That is not true. Some leaders get greedy and manipulative after reaching a high level of achievement. You should not allow them to kill your dreams so that you can satisfy their selfish desires. If they are unwilling to help you fulfil your purpose, just love and leave them; but never give up on your dreams to please them. Some want to overwork you to prevent you from doing your God-given work. Do not give them the chance.

"YOU SHOULD NEVER LET YOU DOWN."

~Nadia McInnis~

Yes, it is up to you and you alone. God has placed it in your control and He is there to help you. Do not let yourself down, work hard on your purpose as if someone has already paid you to get the work done and they are expecting great results.

*"ENCOURAGE YOUR CHILDREN
TO TAKE PART IN COMPETITIONS,
IT INCREASES THEIR CAPACITY
TO RECOVER QUICKLY
FROM DIFFICULTIES."*

~Nadia McInnis~

In my early school days I entered so many competitions from beauty contests to debating competitions, and to my surprise, I am stronger and more resilient than I thought I could ever be. I have also heard people whom I consider to be successful, talk about the competitions they entered and events they took part in when they were younger. It does not matter the results, the fact that you can go on after a loss means you are building resilience.

"ALL HONEST PEOPLE SHOULD STAND UP, SHOW UP, AND TAKE CONTROL."

~Nadia McInnis~

One of the most painful things for me is to see people who hurt others with no remorse appear to be winning and dominating while the good people are quiet and losing.

Evil prevails when good people do nothing, so we, the good people, should stand up, show up and take control. When good people are in power the people rejoice when evil people are in power the people mourn.

"DO NOT FEEL BAD ABOUT WHAT OTHERS SAY BEHIND YOUR BACK. THE BACKDROP IS IMPORTANT TO BOOST YOUR APPEARANCE."

~Nadia McInnis~

I once read a story about a lady who was very loved by the public, when suddenly, she confronted someone publicly on a live show. The public went from adoring her to blind hate. So many people were talking negatively about this lady as they were no longer held back due to her popularity. I decided to find out who this lady was and what had really happened. I have since become a fan and watched her social media page grow to over 100,000 more followers than before people started talking negatively about her. Not all negative stories about you are bad for you; some are for your promotion. In my opinion, this lady's influence increased since that day, despite all the negative commentary.

"SPEND YOUR PRECIOUS TIME WITH P.P.P.'s - POSITIVE, PROGRESSIVE PEOPLE."

~Nadia McInnis~

Birds of a feather flock together. You are like the people you spend most of your time with. Influence is another subtle but sure thing. Positivity is contagious and also is negativity. You will not notice when one of them has consumed the other, so ensure it is positivity.

"SUCCESS IS THE INABILITY TO GIVE UP. FAILURE IS GIVING UP."

~Nadia McInnis~

One major difference between a successful man and a failure is that one gave up and the other did not. They both experienced some sort of defeat. A successful man just refused to give up. He will try all means over and over again until he finds a way because he has persuaded himself, or someone persuaded him, that there is a way. The failure tried and saw no way, so he decided that he had had enough of trying and settled for what is convenient.

"MY PRESENT AND FUTURE ARE SO BRIGHT I NEED SUNGLASSES!"

~Nadia McInnis~

Sometimes, you will feel so excited about the progress you are making that you just have to shout out in joy. You will eventually look back at where you started and be grateful for what you have achieved.

"WHO SAID IT WAS EASY? HE ONLY SAID YOU WILL MAKE IT."

-Nadia McInnis-

No one ever said that there would not be challenges in fulfilling your purpose; no one ever said that there would not be times when you want to give up; no one ever said there would not be times when you sit and cry out of frustration. There will certainly be difficult times but relax - you are going to make it. Just keep doing your best and stay with God.

"THE ROAD TO SUCCESS WILL AT TIMES GET LONELY. DO NOT GIVE UP BEFORE THE FINISH LINE, THERE WILL BE MANY TO CELEBRATE AND GREET YOU AT THE END."

~Nadia McInnis~

Sometimes you will get so lonely that you want to detour. You may want to work with more people believing it would be a better working environment. There might not be many people walking this way with you, but do not worry - there will be many to celebrate and greet you at the end.

"THANK EVERYONE WHO TREATED YOU BADLY WHEN YOU TRUSTED THEM. EVERY SITUATION WILL HELP YOU TO YOUR DESTINATION."

-Nadia McInnis-

Thank everyone who betrayed you and pray for them. They subconsciously pushed you where you are today, and think about it, you are at a good place. You are discovering and fulfilling your purpose. You probably would have died with all your gifts and talents inside of you and not left a legacy. CONGRATULATIONS, AND WELCOME TO LIFE.

*"DO NOT WAIT FOR
OPPORTUNITIES TO PRESENT
THEMSELVES BEFORE YOU,
PRESENT YOURSELF BEFORE
OPPORTUNITIES."*

~Nadia McInnis~

I want you to write this several times in your house, in your office and just everywhere that you go. If you do not look for the opportunities that your business needs no one will bring them to you. The only time people will offer you opportunities is when you have established or are known for your service. So find opportunities until they start finding you.

*"A MAN'S WAYS HAVE NOTHING
TO DO WITH HOW EDUCATED
HE IS. GET TO KNOW SOMEONE'S
PERSONALITY BEFORE YOU
COME TO A CONCLUSION."*

~Nadia McInnis~

When I was a young girl I once believed that very educated people were also people of justice who had good morals. I somehow linked education and achievements to good morals and people of good character. I was so FAR from the real, absolute truth. They have absolutely nothing to do with each other. Whether someone is educated or not, get to know people's character before you come to any conclusions. When an educated wise man is evil he is a very dangerous person.

*"BE STRONG ENOUGH TO RELEASE
NEGATIVITY SO THAT POSITIVITY
CAN COME INTO YOUR LIFE. THEY
CANNOT FUNCTION TOGETHER."*

~Nadia McInnis~

We sometimes like to hold on to negative people or behaviours because it is convenient, familiar and comfortable. But in order to be successful you must get rid of it. If you don't, one will suppress the other, and if most of your life you have been living the negative life, most likely that one will dominate. Get rid of negativity altogether.

"YOU ARE NOT A FAILURE, YOU BECOME A FAILURE WHEN YOU BELIEVE THOSE WHO DON'T BELIEVE IN YOU."

-Nadia McInnis-

You should not take advice from everyone who offers it. I do not care what they have achieved or who they are. Do not take everyone's advice. Some people know how to gain personal achievement but have no clue as to how to help others achieve theirs. While there are also some who know how to help others achieve but are too selfish to share their information with anyone. They will even try to talk you out of the little you know and make it seem irrelevant. They are insignificant where your progress is concerned.

"JUST BECAUSE THEY LAUGH WITH YOU OR SAY THAT THEY LIKE YOU DOESN'T MEAN THAT THEY WANT YOU TO PROGRESS. WHAT DO THEY DO WHEN YOU PROGRESS?"

~Nadia McInnis~

Sometimes it is good to stop listening to the many talks and start watching the walk. Take note of people's actions more than their words. I have discovered that people can and are willing to say anything to get what they want from you, but what are they really doing? That is what you should ask yourself. Are they helping when they can or are they just telling you what you want to hear to get what they want?

"IF YOU ARE CRYING AND FRUSTRATED ABOUT THE SAME OLD STORY, BEGIN A NEW STORY TODAY. DOING NOTHING WILL NOT CHANGE A THING."

~Nadia McInnis~

So many people stay in a negative situation and just cry day after day hoping that the situation will change by itself. It does not matter the situation you are in, change will not happen until you make it happen. You have to bring the change that is required. Stop crying and change the situation.

*"SOME OF THE PEOPLE YOU
ARE WAITING TO HELP YOU
FULFIL YOUR DREAMS ARE NOT
THE ONES TO HELP YOU. OPEN
YOUR HEART TO RECEIVE HELP
ELSEWHERE, DO NOT LIMIT GOD."*

~Nadia McInnis~

If you have not already discovered this, you will soon discover this as you fulfil your purpose. When this happens, just learn the lesson and keep going. People whom you least expect help and support from will sometimes support you more than the ones you expected it from. Some of your helpers may be strangers. Take the help from those who are willing, forgive those who didn't help you and keep doing. God can and will use anyone so don't put all your eggs in one basket.

*"NEVER ASSUME THAT
BECAUSE SOMEONE IS ALWAYS
ASKING YOU FOR SOMETHING
THEY ARE WILLING TO DO
THE SAME FOR YOU."*

~Nadia McInnis~

Simply put, do not make any assumptions as to what you think someone will do for you. It is easy to believe that because you always support them they will automatically return the favour. I have discovered that there are far more selfish people in the world than kind people. Do not put your future in the hands of any man. The Bible says that men kept talking about how good Jesus was but He never gave himself to them because he knew their hearts.

"SOMETIMES YOU NEED TO CHANGE YOUR ENVIRONMENT SO THAT YOU DON'T GET CHANGED BY YOUR ENVIRONMENT."

~Nadia McInnis~

Have you ever been a part of an organization and you are patiently waiting for it to get better, waiting for a better leader or for justice to be served but it never happens? You keep praying for change but instead grow more irritable and frustrated.

You know that it will not be long before you explode, which would be a disaster. In this case, just kindly change your environment and keep your dignity.

"WHEN YOU KNOW YOU ARE BACKED BY A BIG GOD YOU HAVE A FEARLESS BOLDNESS TO CONQUER GIANTS."

~Nadia McInnis~

You should aim to get to the point in your life where you know that your God is too big for any human to stop you or what He has planned for your life. When you get to that stage, you do not give any attention to their noise and lies because you are assured that God will defeat them for you. Not that God does not love us all, God loves us all but some people have decided, through their actions, that they hate God and they want to try and destroy His people and His plans. He has to fight for you because He told you that the battle is not YOURS but HIS, right?

"GO WHERE YOU CAN GROW."

~Nadia McInnis~

Some places and under some leaders there is no growth because they are not true leaders, they are dictators. Their only mission is to keep you followers as their errand children. You will know them because they will never support your dreams or try to help you fulfil YOUR assignment. They might pretend to get what they want, but eventually, they will be exposed. Get out from under them, they are dream killers. It is all about them and what they can achieve and how you should help them get there. If you don't help them you are in trouble so get out from under them and do not let them make you bitter by killing your passion and purpose.

"TRUE LEADERS DON'T JUST KNOW WHAT TO DO, THEY DO WHAT THEY KNOW."

~Nadia McInnis~

Some leaders are experts on telling people what to do and how to do it. In fact, they are the first to correct and reprimand. But you watch them when they are in the same situation as you were, they will not even attempt to do a fraction of the things they commanded you to do and no one can speak to them about it because they use their position as a defence. They are not true leaders, they are manipulators. Anyone with a gift that they want to share should not be under them because they will bury it.

*"SOME PEOPLE ONLY APPRECIATE
AND RESPECT THOSE WHO STAND
UP TO THEM AND CHALLENGE
THEM. TOLERANT AND FRIENDLY
PEOPLE ARE MOSTLY TREATED
UNFAIRLY AND DISRESPECTED.
START TO SET BOUNDARIES
TO PROTECT YOUR JOY."*

~Nadia McInnis~

You shouldn't be quiet at all times; there is a time to talk. I have observed that once who know better but are too afraid to speak up you will eventually suffer along with others. It is as if there is a punishment for not speaking up when you had the chance to do so. Unfortunately, things will not change until you do something, at least do what you can do and leave the rest to God.

*"TO GET WHAT OTHERS HAVE,
OR TO GET MORE THAN OTHERS
HAVE, IS NOT TO HATE AND
TELL LIES ABOUT THEM, BUT TO
LOVE AND APPRECIATE THEM."*

~Nadia McInnis~

You must love and appreciate those who have achieved what you want to achieve. Hating and telling lies on them stops you from getting to where they are.

Never think that you can get from God what others have by telling lies on those people whom God has blessed. The blessings of God do not work like that. What you sow you will reap, so, sow love, sow truth, sow thanksgiving and appreciation and you will reap the same, or even better, blessings.

"THERE ARE MANY TALKERS. PAY ATTENTION TO WHAT THEY DO NOT WHAT THEY SAY. THIS WILL SAVE YOU A LOT OF TROUBLE."

~Nadia McInnis~

No one could have convinced me before that if someone sounded very sincere and genuine about something that they may not mean what they say.

Some people are so good at deception; they are first class liars and PHD deceiver holders. The only way to find these people out is to watch their actions. They say actions speak louder than words and it is true, but sometimes we are so drawn in by their fantastic talking that we do not even see that they are doing the opposite of what they are saying. Pay attention to people's actions more than what they say and it will save you disappointment.

"EVERYONE HAS A GIFT AND THE POWER TO SHOW IT."

~Nadia McInnis~

Every person has something that they were born to do and God gave every man the ability to accomplish their purpose on earth. It is up to you to start and allow God to sustain and guide you as you discover and maximize your gift.

"IF SOMEONE COPIES YOUR IDEA, DO NOT LEAVE YOUR LANE AND CRASH. AT THE END, THE ONE WITH THE PASSION AND DETERMINATION WILL SUCCEED."

~Nadia McInnis~

You will see other people copying your ideas and trying to be you and that is ok. It shows that you have something special because others want to be like you. Use it as motivation. Do not stop what you are doing to copy them back or to copy another person. Run your own race and stick to what you are supposed to do.

"HOLD NO MAN HIGH ENOUGH TO LET HIM TALK YOU OUT OF WHAT GOD HAS CALLED YOU TO DO."

-Nadia McInnis-

Too many people get bitter because they allow people who called themselves leaders, and people they trusted, talk them out of doing what they know God told them to do. Always remember that it is better to please God than man; the men you try to please will one day try to destroy you. Please God always and no man will be able to stand against you all the days of your life.

"A LOT OF PEOPLE ARE WEALTHY AND UNHAPPY. YOUR GIFT WILL BRING YOU JOY AND FORTUNE."

~Nadia McInnis~

Do you see how many famous people with money commit suicide or are on drugs? Money alone is not what brings you complete happiness. What brings you joy is finding out your God-given assignment, working on it excellently and being rewarded while other important aspects of life are in order.

"NOTHING CAN STOP A MAN WHO IS HONEST, WISE, WORKS HARD AND KNOWS GOD."

~Nadia McInnis~

Nothing can stop that man but himself. No matter how things appear around me, my confidence is always that the God who created heaven and earth is big enough to take me through stronger and better than I was before. Just trust in God and in His power because no human can stop what He started unless you have consciously or subconsciously allowed them to. But even after being side-tracked, you can turn things around for your good by allowing God to guide you.

"WITHOUT A PLAN YOUR DREAMS WILL REMAIN IN YOUR HEAD AND IN YOUR BED."

~ Nadia McInnis~

Planning before action will drastically improve your life. It does not matter how gifted and talented you are, if you do not plan your daily assignments to accomplish what you want, you will not achieve as much. You can achieve so much, and go so far if you just plan out your days. Plan how you will conquer the mountains you want to face before you start climbing. As you pass a milestone, cross it off and keep going. Ensure that you have fun every step of the way but start by writing down your daily tasks.

"WHATEVER YOU ALLOW TO HAPPEN TO YOU IS UP TO YOU."

~Nadia McInnis~

Be bold and confident to ask for what you want and tell people what you do not want. I will say it again; there is no reward for being quiet when you are hurting - unless God told you to be quiet. It is best to let people know the wrong they are doing to you instead of telling it to someone else. You will feel fulfilled and they will respect you more if they are decent people.

"WHEN YOU NOTICE SOMETHING GOOD ABOUT A FRIEND TELL THEM SO THAT THEY CAN BUILD ON IT. THEY WILL ALWAYS REMEMBER."

~Nadia McInnis~

A true friend should tell other friends, not just the things they need to improve, but also the things that they are good at. A good friend should tell you more of those good things so that they can build on them instead of using every opportunity to emphasise on the negative things about you. You do not want to be around those people, they are energy drainers and joy killers.

"SOMETIMES THE THINGS YOU NEED ARE STARING YOU IN THE FACE, WHEN YOU ARE READY YOU WILL FIND THEM."

~Nadia McInnis~

I have heard people say that when the student is ready then the teacher will show up. The teacher has always been available, but the student cannot see him or even appreciate him because they do not know what they really want. As soon as you are serious about what you want to achieve, and are ready to take action, you will see opportunities everywhere - even in your community and times of relaxation.

*"DON'T LET PEOPLE PULL
YOU INTO THEIR BATTLES.
YOU SHOULD BE CONFIDENT
IN WHAT YOU KNOW."*

~Nadia McInnis~

So many times, I see people with a little authority trying to influence those who listen to them to do the wrong things. They know that some of the people who follow them are vulnerable and are not thinking for themselves. They successfully persuade their followers to do the wrong thing convincing them that it is the right thing to do.

We should be confident in what we know and use our brains to reason things out for ourselves. Do not just follow everything someone said because they have been right or good to you a few times. Reason things out logically and do not be influenced negatively to please others. There is no reward for not using your brain.

"THINK PURE THOUGHTS AND REMAIN FOCUSED ON YOUR DREAMS AND GREAT IDEAS WILL COME TO YOU."

~Nadia McInnis~

Thinking pure thoughts and giving thanks to God is of utmost importance for shining your light. The kind of extraordinary ideas that will come to you are unfathomable. The devil will always try to lead your mind back to the hurt, rejections and disappointments, but if you remember that you want to live the best life you will fight the fight in your mind and keep thinking pure thoughts. Great ideas will come to you and then you should act upon them. One of the things you can do is say, "Thank you, Jesus" every time a negative thought comes to you and keep repeating it until it goes away.

"DO NOT STAY IN THE PRESENCE OF THOSE WHO ARE ALWAYS TELLING YOU WHAT IS WRONG WITH YOU AND MAKING A MOUNTAIN OF FAILURES."

~Nadia McInnis~

These things are subtle but detrimental to your growth. You will not know when you lose your passion and your self-confidence. If you have a problem and you get to know about it say thank you very much and start to change yourself. You do not need anyone to bring up your mistakes or problems every time you meet them. That will make you bitter and too conscious of your weaknesses - not better. Most of these people are struggling with the problems they keep talking about and it makes them feel better to say it is someone else's weakness.

"STOP WASTING YOUR PRECIOUS TIME TRYING TO PLEASE THE WRONG PEOPLE. GIVE YOUR TIME AND ENERGY TO THOSE WHO APPRECIATE YOU. APPRECIATION STRENGTHENS A MAN WHILE DISREGARD WEAKENS HIM."

-Nadia McInnis-

You will never be able to please some people, even if you give them your life they want to take your children's lives also. When you discover this, just leave them alone and associate with people who appreciate you in words and actions. Everything else is destroying your energy.

*"YOUNG PEOPLE DO NOT WAIT
FOR YOUR MENTORS TO TELL
YOU IF YOU ARE GIFTED OR
TO SUPPORT YOUR DREAMS.
YOUR GIFT WAS GIVEN TO YOU
BY GOD, LISTEN TO HIM."*

~Nadia McInnis~

Do not wait for people you look up to, to tell you how great you are and how much potential you have for you to recognize that you are great.

*"NEVER CONDEMN A PERSON
WITHOUT FIRST TRYING TO
FIND OUT THE PROBLEM OR
TRYING TO HELP HIM."*

~Nadia McInnis~

Many people have experienced things that they are struggling to overcome. If you are unsure of their actions then the best thing to do is to try and find out why they are doing what you think or heard that they are doing. Do not condemn them or judge them. You never know until you ask and try to find out the reasons behind their actions.

"IF YOU CAN MASTER YOUR MIND YOU WILL MASTER YOUR LIFE."

~Nadia McInnis~

You will be very surprised at how powerful your mind is. Once you get a hold of it and control what you think about, you will have control over your actions. They say as a man thinks so is he - let me explain that for you. It means that whatever you spend the most time thinking about, you will begin to see ways, behave in ways or find ways to acquire those things which should propel you to do it or become it. If you know how you want to live your life you should know what you should be thinking about.

"ALLOW YOUR MIND TO CREATE YOUR BIGGEST DREAMS. THINK IT AND DO IT."

-Nadia McInnis-

Allow your mind to create what you want, do not limit yourself and think that anything is too good or too high for you to achieve. Think about it then do it. The more you think about it, the more ways you will discover how to do it.

"OBSTACLES FORCE YOU TO GROW, DON'T MOAN - GET BIGGER."

~Nadia McInnis~

Don't moan, get bigger. If there are people trying to block you just get bigger than them so that they are no longer a hindrance. They can only block you if you are under them and they have some control over you. If you get bigger and come away from them, they have no power over you.

"THE DAYS OF DREAMING ARE OVER, IT IS ACTION TIME NOW. SO, GET UP, DRESS UP AND SHOW UP AND NEVER GIVE UP UNTIL YOU ARE UP."

~Nadia McInnis~

You need to get up, dress up and show up, never giving up until you are up in heaven with the Lord. It is OK to dream so you can have a vision of where you want to be. But after that, get to work and don't stop working until your work on earth is done. There are pleasure and peace in this kind of work.

"EVERYWHERE YOU GO, IN EVERYTHING YOU DO, LET YOUR LIGHT SHINE SO BRIGHT SO THAT OTHERS HAVE TO ASK YOU ABOUT YOUR LIFE."

~Nadia McInnis~

The Bible says that we should let our light shine for ALL TO SEE and GLORIFY our Father who is in heaven. It is your responsibility to shine your light everywhere you go so that God can be glorified. You make it happen.

"WHEN GOD SAYS 'LET ME HANDLE IT' JUST LET HIM. HE WILL DO IT BETTER THAN YOU."

~Nadia McInnis~

So many times people want to fight their own battles, but God says the battle is not yours, it is the Lords. God is not a bully so if you insist on fighting your own battle He will allow you to but let me assure you that you will not win. If He fights it for you, then you are guaranteed victory. It does not matter how big, how skilful or how many opponents you have, you are guaranteed victory if you give the battle to God. Is there anything too difficult for God?

"WHEN YOU BEGIN TO LOVE AND RESPECT YOURSELF, YOU NEED A NEW CONTACT LIST."

~Nadia McInnis~

Yes, that is right, because many of the people that you were with when you did not respect or value yourself were only with you because you respected and valued them instead of yourself. They love what you do to them, and for them, and they do not want you to stop.

The moment you decide to give yourself some credit and do something to make yourself better, some will turn against you. This is a blessing, not a curse because you now know that with them you were not going anywhere.

"IF YOU DON'T KNOW THE SCRIPTURES, YOU WILL PAY"

~Nadia McInnis~

I have seen and heard many people twist the scriptures to benefit themselves or to get what they want from people. Some of these people are very persuasive and if you do not know the scriptures for yourself you will do all they tell you to do even though the scriptures are clearly against it. The Bible tells us to study to show ourselves approved unto God. God also said that my people are destroyed for lack of knowledge.

You should read the word of God for yourself so when your leaders echo it you have already read, meditated and understood it. When you do this, you will know when they have twisted it to suit their own needs. Make it an assignment to read and meditate on the entire Bible every year, so someone taking one or two scriptures and twisting it, will not deceive you. Do not be destroyed for lack of knowledge.

*"FIRST YOU ARE BROKEN,
THEN IT LOOKS LIKE THEY
REBUILD YOU. THEN THEY
MANIPULATE YOU, THEN YOU
GET FRUSTRATED. THEN YOU
CHOOSE TO LIVE OR DIE."*

~Nadia McInnis~

Some people are experts in looking for broken people to give them false hope, so that they can manipulate and mistreat them.

If this has happened to you, the thing to do now is to choose to live and shine your light because you are far more knowledgeable and experienced.

"CLEAN OUT YOUR SURROUNDINGS IN PREPARATION FOR YOUR DESTINATION."

~Nadia McInnis~

Clear out every bad acquaintance, every negative conversation and everything which leads you astray if you are serious about living a better life. A new and bright destiny requires good company, positive conversation and a good support system to help you get there. There will be challenges along the way but when you have the right things, people, and mindset, it will be easier for you to deal with them.

"THE SAME ADVERSITY THAT WAS MEANT TO DESTROY YOU CAN BE USED FOR YOUR VICTORY."

~Nadia McInnis~

Do not be afraid of adversaries, they cannot stop your progress. Stop and look at them, you will see that they have no power except that which you give them. Use them as motivation to move higher and as examples to explain to others how weak and powerless they are.

"IF GOD IS IN YOUR BUSINESS YOU WILL EVENTUALLY DISCOVER THAT EVERYTHING YOU HAVE DONE CONSCIOUSLY AND SUBCONSCIOUSLY HAS WORKED OUT FOR YOUR SUCCESS.

~Nadia McInnis~

I remember when I started my first company, I did so many things on a daily basis because I was not sure what to do. I had no human mentor or instructor so I was just doing what I thought was necessary to grow the company and give it publicity. I soon realised that everything I did consciously and subconsciously was very important. I can confidently say that it all contributed to my success today; even those things I thought were insignificant and a waste of my time.

*"PEOPLE CAN ONLY SEE WHAT
YOU SHOW THEM OR WHAT
THEY WANT TO SEE, BUT ONLY
YOU KNOW WHAT IS INSIDE
OF YOU. SO IF WHAT THEY ARE
SEEING IS NOT THE REAL YOU,
MAKE UP YOUR MIND TO START
REFLECTING WHAT IS INSIDE OF
YOU. IT IS YOUR RESPONSIBILITY
TO SHINE YOUR LIGHT."*

~Nadia McInnis~

Of course there are those who choose to see what they want to see and will accept nothing else - even when it is staring them in the face. However, for the ones who want the best for you, make sure you shine your light for ALL to see. If I do not know that you offer a service or have a product which I need then I will not ask for it, so let your gift and talents be known.

*"DO NOT BE INFLUENCED BY
FLATTERY. KNOW YOUR VALUES,
KNOW YOUR MISSION SO THAT
YOU ARE NOT DECEIVED.
NOT EVERY ENEMY COMES
WITH A SWORD, SOME COME
BY FLATTERY, BUT IF YOU
STICK TO YOUR VALUES AND
YOUR MISSION, YOU WILL NOT
FALL INTO THEIR TRAPS."*

-Nadia McInnis-

So many times I have seen people being deceived because they are moved by flattery. They will get rid of the decent, good and loyal people around them simply because someone else came flattering and deceiving them. The only end to that relationship is destruction if the one being flattered does not realise the deception soon and take action. Stick to your convictions and the truth and it does not matter how much they flatter you, you will not fall into their trap because you did not compromise.

"IF YOU EVER THINK YOU CAN DEFEAT ME, YOU ARE WASTING YOUR TIME; I AM UNBROKEN, UNCONQUERED, UNDEFEATED AND EXTREMELY BLESSED.

~Nadia McInnis~

One day after reading a section of my book *"A Sister's Pain,"* I came to the conclusion that I am totally undefeated. I read about the many tragedies the young lady encountered and still never gave up but instead aimed higher and got more successful. I then said to myself, 'I would love to meet that lady because she is indeed one of a kind.'

It does not matter what you have been through or the mistakes you have made if you walk with God, He will turn everything around for your good.

WHATEVER YOU DECIDE TO DO, DECIDE TO BECOME THE BEST AT IT.

~Nadia McInnis~

Do not accept mediocrity in your life, if you decide to be a singer be the best singer, if you decide to be a speaker become the best speaker, if you decide to be a teacher, become the best teacher. Study the best in your area, learn something from them and add your uniqueness to what you discover. Become the greatest. You have it in you so do it.

"IF YOU MUST START ALONE, THEN START, BUT WHATEVER YOU DO, DON'T GIVE UP ON YOUR DREAMS."

~Nadia McInnis~

I know they say that alone you can run fast but together you can run farther but I am telling you that when you start your mission, you might not have anyone to start with you or even have someone who believes in you. Do not worry, start by yourself. As you are on your way you will see and invite the people who are there to help you. Do not wait for them to show up before you start, just start by yourself.

"SOME WILL GIVE YOU A
FREE VIRUS SO THAT THEY
CAN SELL YOU A CURE."

~Nadia McInnis~

There is a big difference between correcting someone in love and allowing them to grow than constantly trying to lower someone's self-esteem and confidence. They do this to the point where people treat them as their God and a know-it-all so that they can manipulate people. Don't allow anyone, irrespective of position, to talk down to you and make you believe that you are nothing without them. This is abuse and manipulation.

"SOMETIMES YOU MIGHT NOT KNOW HOW GREAT YOUR IDEAS ARE UNTIL OTHERS START TO COPY THEM."

~Nadia McInnis~

As soon as you start to shine your light you will see many people who never encouraged or supported you begin to copy you. Some will even be successful in doing so. The important thing is not to let it worry or trouble you. Just keep doing what you are doing. Keep learning, improving and growing. Become the best but never let it bother you or distract you. As soon as you start to act big all the small actors will wake up.

"YOU CAN'T REACH YOUR DESTINATION IF YOU KEEP GOING BACK."

~Nadia McInnis~

There is no progress in going back to the past. Only use the past to help people in that situation to get out. Let your future become more important than your past. Do not go back to abusers or the people who pushed you towards your destination by abusing you. If you return to them you cannot get to your destination. You need new associations for your new mission. If they were good for you why didn't you make any progress with your purpose around them? Look to the future and see the new open doors and opportunities.

"YOU WILL ENCOUNTER SEVERAL TEMPORARY OBSTACLES TOWARDS YOUR DESTINATION. DO NOT FOCUS ON THEM, REMAIN FOCUSED AND THOSE OBSTACLES WILL BECOME CHEERLEADERS."

-Nadia McInnis-

Forget and move on from people and situations that try to hinder you as you progress. Do not allow any of them to take your mind off your destiny, because if they succeed in taking your mind off your destiny, they have succeeded in taking your eyes off your destiny. Your success is down to the actions you take so stay focused, do not get distracted and watch those obstacles become cheerleaders.

"AMAZING THINGS HAPPEN TO YOU WHEN YOU BELIEVE IN YOU."

-Nadia McInnis-

You must believe in yourself to live a truly successful life. When you start to believe in yourself you will notice that situations and people react to you differently. Do not act like you are a beggar or disadvantaged because you are not. Practice being confident when talking to people, keep practicing until you have mastered it and watch how amazing doors will open for you.

"STOP COMPLAINING AND LOOK THE LION IN THE FACE, YOU WILL SEE THAT IT IS TOOTHLESS."

~Nadia McInnis~

As you run towards your destiny do not get intimidated by anyone irrespective of their position or influence. They may not like what you are doing but God is backing you so you are protected by the greatest. Do not be afraid of them, your success is guaranteed. Look them in the eyes and see that they are empty and so are their words.

*"YOU MUST ALWAYS REMEMBER
THAT HATE AND EVIL DO
NOT SPECIALIZE IN ANYONE.
THE BEST THING TO DO IS TO
SHUN EVILDOERS BECAUSE IT
IS ONLY A MATTER OF TIME
BEFORE IT IS YOUR TIME."*

~Nadia McInnis~

Never help anyone try to destroy another man's reputation or tell lies on anyone. Never do that. The same people who encourage and send you to do evil to another will do worse to you. It is only a matter of time. I watched a film where a crime boss had a hired hitman, he had this man killing for him - even members of the killers own family. When the guy offended him that same boss tried to kill everything connected to his killer including the killer himself. It is no different with anyone who sends you to do evil.

"YOU WILL NEVER SEE OR HEAR ME JOIN AN EVIL PERSON TO PERSECUTE AN INNOCENT PERSON. ONE - IT IS WRONG AND TWO - YOUR TIME IS FAST APPROACHING."

~Nadia McInnis~

I have explained it all before but I am saying it again another way for those who did not get it; this is very important.

*"DO NOT ALLOW UNNECESSARY
CHURCH ACTIVITIES TO DISTRACT
YOU FROM YOUR PURPOSE ON
EARTH. SO MANY PEOPLE ARE
SUFFERING TODAY WITH NO
ONE TO TURN TO BUT GOD.
YOUR MAIN ACTIVITY SHOULD
BE TO DISCOVER YOUR PURPOSE
AND SHINE YOUR LIGHT FOR
THE WORLD TO SEE - NOT BE
LOST IN A CONGREGATION."*

-Nadia McInnis-

It is good to volunteer your services in the church, I did it for several years and discovered my love for helping young people there. But there comes a time when some of you know that you are called to go worldwide and help people outside the four walls of the church. When this time comes you will know because you will feel limited. Many leaders will not like it and will try to destroy your life but if you hold on to God and do exactly what He says you will be the one standing tall at the end of the day.

*"LEARNING FROM SOMEONE
SHOULD NOT MEAN THAT YOU
HAVE TO GIVE UP YOUR DREAMS
TO FOLLOW THEM. A TRUE LEADER
WILL NOT ASK YOU TO ABANDON
YOUR GOD-GIVEN ASSIGNMENT."*

~Nadia McInnis~

It is time for each person to understand that they have their own unique gift and skills that they need to use to build their own enterprise. It is ok to learn from other people and help them out when you can but do not, I repeat do not, give up on your own assignment to focus completely on theirs.

Do not put your assignment to one side to develop these people's dreams because if they allow you to do that in the first place chances are that when they become successful you will not be a part of their success.

*"IF SOMEONE ASKS YOU TO GIVE
UP YOUR DREAMS TO FOLLOW
THEIRS, ASK THEM TO GIVE UP
THEIRS TO FOLLOW YOURS."*

~Nadia McInnis~

Can you see the hard work they put into accomplishing their mission? Do the same and more for YOURS, but don't let them talk you out of your dreams. Even if they are your leaders they should know better. You may be small and slow in your progress but every big business was once a small business. Some people will tell you that because you are inexperienced you need their experience. If you need to learn from them that is fine, only, give yourself a time limit and do not abort your dreams.

"IT DOESN'T MATTER HOW MANY TIMES YOU DECLARE IT IS GOING TO BE A GREAT YEAR NOTHING WORKS UNTIL YOU WORK IT."

~Nadia McInnis~

Without a great plan and better action you will always remain the same. Declaration and meditation are good but it should cause you to do what you want to do. That is the reason behind meditation and declarations.

"THE MOMENT YOU DECIDE TO DREAM AND ACT BIG YOU WILL DISCOVER THAT SOME CLOSE FRIENDS WERE CLOSE ENEMIES."

~Nadia McInnis~

Fulfilling your purpose is the fastest and best way to get rid of the previously unknown negativity out of your life. Enemies will start to spring up from everywhere, even those who said they were your best friends. Just thank God that you now know them, love them and leave them alone.

*"SEPARATE YOURSELF FROM
PEOPLE'S OPINIONS AND
BECOME THE GREAT PERSON
YOU KNOW YOU ARE."*

~Nadia McInnis~

Everyone has an opinion about something, but not everyone's opinion is useful or important to you. Let them keep their opinions and you keep making progress.

"DO NOT PUT YOUR HOPE IN MAN, PUT YOUR HOPE IN GOD."

~Nadia McInnis~

Men always disappoint. It does not matter who they are or what they have. If your trust is in God, then you will not be too disappointed in man because you did not put your trust in them anyway.

"WHEN YOU START FULFILLING YOUR PURPOSE SOME PEOPLE WILL ABANDON THEIR OWN PURPOSE JUST TO COPY YOU."

~Nadia McInnis~

Ensure that you are doing what you were born to do because that is where you will shine. Do not divert from your calling and copy someone else's calling because you will not shine there. You have your own purpose, find out what it is and shine.

*"IF GOD IS YOUR COACH YOU
ARE ALREADY A CHAMPION. YOU
CAN NEVER BE DEFEATED."*
~Nadia McInnis~

Make God your number one mentor and coach and everyone else is second.

ACKNOWLEDGEMENTS

I would like to thank the Almighty God, who is my Father, my teacher, my friend, my instructor, my provider, my protector, my love, and my everything. Everything good that I have achieved is because of God. There is nothing great that I have done that was not done because of God in my life and I want to say thank you Lord, you are my life and I would never want to live without you.

I would like to thank my darling husband Obinna Aniagolu whom God has used to be my push. You are just amazing and you have made me a very happy wife and mother. I love you very much.

I would like to thank my best friend Dr Bothwell Xavier, whom God has used to help me prosper and move from glory to glory. Your impact and contribution to my life is something that everyone would want to have. You give everything and expect nothing in return. You are way too gracious and giving and I sincerely wish you and your family God's best. I love you dearly.

To Bunmi who first told me to write the quote book, thank you very much, God bless you.

To my Lovely editor Melissa Hercules, thank you very much. You are so efficient, hard-working and reliable. God bless you.

To all my family and friends, including my two extraordinary blessed children Prince and Princess, I love you all.

OTHER BOOKS BY THE AUTHOR

1. A Sister's Pain
2. Becoming your best